ASIA

Junior Science Books are dedicated to all children who are eager to know more about nature and the world they live in. Written especially for young readers, each Junior Science Book has been carefully tested by the Spache Readability Formula. The purpose of this evaluation is to assure that each book can be read by primary grade children and enjoyed by young readers through the elementary grades.

Junior Science Books are edited and designed under the supervision of Nancy Larrick, Ed.D.

Junior Science Book of

Elephants

By
William D. Sheldon

Illustrated by
Matthew Kalmenoff

THE GARRARD PRESS
Champaign, Illinois

To my daughter Mary Jane,
a great admirer of elephants

The author and editor are grateful to
George G. Goodwin, Associate Curator in the
Department of Mammology, The American Museum
of Natural History, for reading the manuscript
of this book and checking its scientific accuracy.

Contents

In Elephant Country

The first elephant I ever saw was a circus elephant. Before the show, my father took me to the elephant tent. We saw the men scrubbing the elephants and feeding them. We listened to the shrill noises of the great animals.

Later we watched the elephants in the ring. Like every boy in the big tent, I fell in love with elephants. After that I saw every circus parade, not once but twice. I got up early to see the elephants march off the circus train. I read every book I could find about elephants. I was a real elephant fan. At least, I thought I was.

But a few years ago I learned to know elephants in real elephant country. I lived in Cambodia, a small country in southeast Asia. I was in the land of the elephants.

In Cambodia, you see elephants everywhere. They work on farms and in the forests. The Cambodians ride elephants the way our great-grandparents rode horseback. They go to town by elephant. They carry their farm products to market by elephant.

Teams which spray to kill mosquitoes ride on elephants. When men go out to hunt tigers, they ride elephants. The King keeps many elephants on the palace grounds.

In Cambodia I lived near the King's Palace. I often walked to the palace grounds to see the royal elephants.

In Cambodia, you see elephants everywhere.

Each elephant is cared for by his mahout. Every day the mahouts march their elephants through the gates of the palace grounds. Each mahout sits easily on his elephant. He is sure his pet is the best of the lot.

Down the street they walk in single file.

7

Thus the elephants get their exercise around the city of Phnom Penh.

This happens every day. And every day people stop to watch the elephants go by. Children shout and wave to the mahouts. They follow the elephants down the street. No one seems to get tired of watching elephants.

I felt the same way. Day after day, I stood on the street to see the elephants parade. Soon I got to know certain ones. There was the tall dark one with the fierce look in his eye. I always watched for him and for the littlest elephant, who brought up the rear.

On holidays the elephants were dressed up with all sorts of ornaments. Each one carried a beautifully decorated basket on his back. In the basket sat two or three dancing girls. The elephants carried the

Elephants carry dancers to the royal party.

dancers to the place where they danced for the royal party.

Wherever I would go in Cambodia, I watched for elephants. One day I saw a mother elephant and her baby cross the road in front of me. They swung easily into the tall grass and disappeared. There was no need to hurry. Elephants know they are among friends in Cambodia.

In the ancient country of Laos, there are many elephants, too. And everywhere the people of Laos love their elephants.

But I found the children of Laos were troubled. They had seen the American movie about Dumbo the elephant. Dumbo was pink, you remember. And he used his big ears to fly.

One day when I visited a school in Laos, the children asked me about Dumbo. "Are all elephants in the United States pink?" they asked. "Can they all fly like Dumbo?"

The Ancestors of Elephants

Nearly sixty million years ago the ancestors of elephants roamed the earth. That was after the last dinosaurs had disappeared. But it was long before the first men.

These early beasts were not so large as elephants today. In fact, they were only about three feet tall, or the size of a large collie dog.

The first one we know about had a long

11

neck and long head. His trunk was very short. Modern elephants have two tusks, of course. But some of their ancestors had four tusks.

As the years passed, these animals changed in many ways. One kind had no tusks on his upper jaw, but two on his lower jaw. Those long tusks curved backward and downward.

Imperial
mammoth

Another kind had a long lower jaw and a great many teeth. But he had no real trunk.

One ancestor of the elephant lived 30 million years ago. He looked very much like the elephant today. He was very tall. He had two tusks and a long strong trunk. Like the modern elephant, he could touch the ground with that great swinging trunk.

No man ever saw one of these early beasts. For there were no men in that day. Then how do we know what they looked like?

We know from their bones. Scientists have found the remains of these bones. And from them, they have pieced the story together.

A bone seems hard and heavy. But when you look closely, you see it is full of holes. Some are very tiny.

Suppose an animal dies near a stream. Water washes over it. The tiny holes in each bone are filled with water. And water contains minerals.

Or suppose the animal sinks in the mud and dies. Muddy water covers the skeleton. The bones become filled with sand and minerals. Gradually the bones dissolve. They are replaced by mineral deposits.

After thousands of years, these bones are are as hard as concrete. They look like stone and feel like stone, and all stones are mineral. They are called fossils.

In Arizona you can see trees that have become fossils. The great trunks look like pieces of rock. A Connecticut farmer found a stone with dinosaur footprints. These tracks once were in fresh mud. But the mud became a fossil after millions of years.

Many fossils of prehistoric elephant bones have been found. Some show their teeth or tusks. Some show parts of the skeleton. By piecing the parts together, scientists have learned about different kinds of prehistoric elephants.

Fossil footprints

Hairy mammoth

Prehistoric Elephants in Europe and North America

Today wild elephants are found only in Africa and Asia. But long ago they wandered over Europe and North America, too. Eventually they got to South America. Fossils of early elephants have been found in all these places.

Scientists believe that the first elephants lived in Asia. At that time Asia and North

16

America were connected. A strip of land joined them where the Bering Strait lies today. It was called a land bridge.

Animals could walk overland from Asia to North America. Probably the first elephants came to America that way.

One of these early elephants was the mammoth. Often he is called the hairy mammoth because of his long shaggy coat. Some mammoths grew to be 13 feet tall. Their curved tusks were often 12 feet long.

The mammoth probably came to North America about a million years ago. Before ice destroyed the land bridge, herds of mammoths roamed as far south as Minnesota. Probably they died out about 25,000 years ago.

Even so, we know a great deal about mammoths. And, believe it or not, there are people alive who have eaten mammoth

meat. The meat had been frozen, of course,
frozen for thousands of years.

Explorers were studying the ice fields of
northern Asia. In the ice, they found several
complete mammoths, woolly coats and all.
Evidently the great beasts had been caught
in the ice and frozen to death. The meat
was dry and stringy. But freezing had kept
it from spoiling.

Probably early men in America hunted
the mammoth. Indian stories tell of hunting
a beast with long tusks. That may have
been the mammoth, but we don't know.

18

Prehistoric cave paintings of mammoths.

Pictures of mammoths were drawn by early cave men in Europe. In one cave in France, there are 14 different drawings of mammoths. In another, we can see a large picture of two mammoths and two hunters.

One of the most interesting pictures is on a small piece of ivory tusk. It shows a charging mammoth. This carving was found in a cave where ancient men must have lived. There are no mammoths today. But we can study them in the pictures drawn by cave men.

Elephants Today

There are two types of elephants living today. The one you see in the circus is probably an Asian elephant. This one is best known to man. In some places, he has become man's best worker.

The Asian elephant is found in India, Siam, Burma, Laos, Cambodia, Ceylon, Malaya and Sumatra. Sometimes he is called the Indian elephant.

The other kind of elephant lives only in Africa, chiefly in the forests. This is the African elephant.

In many ways the Asian elephant and the African elephant are alike. Both are very large. Both have a long trunk and tusks in the upper jaw. Their heavy gray hide looks wrinkled and loose. You almost think an elephant's skin is a size too big.

If you could see an Asian elephant beside an African elephant, you would see many differences, too. The Asian elephant is about 8 to 10 feet tall. The African elephant is 10 or 11 feet tall and looks heavier and stronger.

In many ways the African elephant is larger. His ears may be as much as 3½ feet across. His tusks may be 10 feet long. Just one tusk may weigh 150 to 200 pounds. Sometimes an elephant will prop his tusks against a tree. It seems to be his way of resting from the great weight.

The African elephant looks bulkier because his shoulders are very high. They seem to make a hump just back of his head. The Asian elephant's back arches where the African elephant's back seems to sag. He has a straighter forehead, too.

African elephant

The skin of an Asian elephant is a light gray. It seems to be smoother than the African elephant's. The heavy dark hide of the African elephant helps him stand the hot sun of his native land.

The most remarkable thing about the elephant is his trunk. He can wrap it around a small tree trunk and pull up the

Asian elephant

tree, roots and all. Or he can pick up a small stick and use it to scratch his back. Perhaps you have seen an elephant pick a peanut out of the grass and toss it in his mouth.

The mother elephant uses her trunk to pat her baby. On the trail she guides him with her trunk. But if her little one needs punishment, he may get a spanking with that same trunk.

If flies bother an elephant, he will pick up dust with his trunk and blow it over his back. If the weather is hot, he uses his trunk to give himself a shower.

At work an elephant will pick up a heavy log with his trunk and move it a great distance.

The elephant's trunk is a mass of muscles and sinews. But it is also very tender. In a fight the elephant curls his trunk out of the way.

Some people think an elephant drinks through his trunk, much as you drink milk through a straw. This is not true. The elephant uses his trunk to dip up water. Then he blows the water into his mouth. On a hot day, he will splash it over his back to cool himself. Or just for fun, he will spray another elephant and look the other way.

A full-grown elephant will weigh as much as 12,000 or 14,000 pounds. To support that weight, his legs are heavy and straight, like great posts. An elephant can stand for hours without getting tired. In fact, the African elephant often sleeps standing up. Only when he is sick or hurt, does he get off those great legs. The Asian elephant lies down quite often.

An elephant's foot is nearly round with a great cushion-like hoof. His ankle is like a man's so he moves easily. Watch an elephant in a parade. You will see that he shuffles one foot ahead of the other. He seems to glide instead of walk. This is his only gait. An elephant can not jump or gallop. But he has a long stride. He moves over the ground pretty fast, and he never seems to get tired. He is a good swimmer, too.

The teeth of an elephant are very unusual. The upper cutting tooth on each side grows to great length. These are the tusks. The four grinding teeth are used for chewing. When these wear away, they drop out. But new grinding teeth come to take their place.

The eyes of an elephant are small, red and weepy. So he sees poorly. But he hears very well. And he has a good sense of smell. He knows when an enemy is coming even though he can't see it.

Life in an Elephant Herd

In the wild, elephants like to live with other elephants. Usually they wander from place to place in herds of eight or ten, sometimes 100. Some people think that each herd is a family.

Usually the leader is the largest cow elephant of the herd. The others follow her and obey her. The herd bull has to be very strong to keep his place as master. Sometimes another male elephant will start a fight with the boss. If he loses, his place is taken by the winner.

Then the defeated bull leaves the herd. He goes off alone. Often he becomes violent, plunging through the jungle and charging anything in his path. The herd bull that has been driven out is called a rogue. He can be very dangerous.

Sometimes several small herds will join forces. Then there may be as many as 100 elephants moving together to search for food and water.

In one day, an elephant might eat 1,000 pounds of food. He likes the tender top branches of low trees or small bushes. If the branches of a tree are too high, he may push the tree over. First, he pushes with his great forehead. After two or three pushes to get the tree swinging, he gives a mighty heave. Over goes the tree.

Imagine a herd of African elephants moving through the jungle. The leader is in front, sniffing the trail with her trunk. Behind her come all the others in single file. Old and young, the elephants shuffle ahead in search of food.

An elephant in the jungle must feed day and night to keep its strength and mighty form. There is little time to rest.

A mother elephant usually has just one baby at a time. Once in a while you hear of elephant twins. One female elephant is likely to have as many as four babies in her whole life. A few have eight or more.

When it is time for a mother to have her baby, she leaves the herd. Another female leaves with her. This one acts like a nurse so elephant trainers call her the Auntie. The Auntie stays with the mother elephant until after the baby is born. She

The tiger could make a meal of the baby elephant.

protects the baby elephant and its mother.

Wild animals can tell when a baby elephant is near by. A tiger, for example, knows the baby is easy to kill and deliciously tender.

When the baby is two or three days old, the mother and Auntie take him back to the herd. He is a wabbly little thing about

31

three feet tall. He weighs between 150 and 200 pounds.

The mother guides him so he will stand under her. She reaches down with her trunk to pat him.

At first he has a hard time eating. His trunk is stiff, and it seems to get in his way. Fortunately, his trunk is on one side of his face at this early age. That makes it easier for him to reach his mother's milk. Soon he learns to curl his trunk over his head while he drinks. Much later, he learns to use that wonderful trunk to put food and water in his mouth.

All the while, the mother and Auntie guard the baby carefully. Wild animals are always lurking near by. The great elephants might accidentally knock him down and hurt him.

It doesn't take long, however, for these

older elephants to get to know the new baby. As he grows, he becomes the pet of the herd. All the elephants protect him.

A young elephant grows very slowly. For at least three or four years, he follows his mother, drinking her milk. Even at 15 he is still growing. Some elephants live to be more than 60 years old.

The Great Search for Ivory

For thousands of years, the elephant has been hunted for his tusks. That is because the tusks are made of ivory. And ivory, like gold and rare jewels, brings a high price.

The outside of an elephant's tusk is often dark. But inside it is creamy white. This seems to be the perfect material for fine carving. It has been used for decorations of all kinds.

Perhaps you have seen a chess set carved from ivory. Each figure is like a tiny

34

statue. Every detail is perfect. Piano keys are made of ivory, too. So are fine combs and the handles of some knives and forks.

An interesting piece of carved ivory was found in a cave in southern France. We know that prehistoric men lived in this cave. So we are sure their artists used ivory. Probably it was ivory from the tusks of a mammoth.

Artists in ancient Egypt made carvings on ivory, too. We read that the throne of King Solomon was made of ivory. And in our museums we see ivory carvings of the ancient Greeks, Chinese, and Japanese.

The tusks of the African elephant produce the best ivory. It is lighter in color. And it can take a finer polish. Besides, the tusks of the African elephant are larger than those of the Asian elephant.

In the past, millions of elephants have been killed by ivory hunters. Eagerly they tracked down a great herd. Then they started a ring of fires around the elephants. As the fires spread, the great beasts stampeded. As the elephants rushed to escape, the hunters struck to kill.

In one year, more than 10,000 African elephants were killed by hunters. It looked as though they would destroy every elephant.

Now laws have been passed to protect the elephant. A hunter must get a permit to kill one. The days of killing a whole herd are gone.

But hunters still like to tell tales of the search for ivory. One is the story of finding an elephant graveyard. This is said to be the place where elephants go off to die. In the center is a huge pile of elephant tusks, just waiting for some lucky ivory hunter.

Probably the elephant graveyard exists only in the hunters' dreams. No one has ever seen one. In fact, few hunters have seen the body or tusks of a dead elephant. His flesh is eaten by a great squad of ants, vultures, jackals, and hyenas. His bones are destroyed by forest fires. Or they may be washed away by heavy rains.

Ivory taken from a freshly killed elephant is called *living* ivory. We don't get much of this today.

We do get what is called *dead* ivory. This is ivory that has been stored for many years. Some of it comes from prehistoric animals found in the frozen ground of Siberia. Dead ivory is not considered as fine as living ivory.

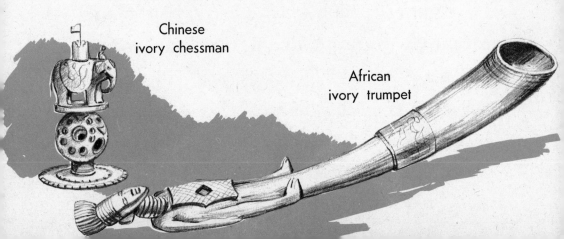

Chinese
ivory chessman

African
ivory trumpet

Big Game Hunting

In both Africa and Asia, elephants are hunted today. But hunters cannot kill any elephant they find. They must have a permit. In many countries, men cannot kill elephants at all. In others, they must pay a big price for a permit.

Men can get a permit to hunt and kill a rogue elephant. He is very dangerous. He will trample down the crops of a village. Or he will attack and kill people who come in his path.

It is not easy to hunt a rogue elephant. He travels slowly, at about four miles an hour. And he leaves a broad trail. So it is easy to follow him. But the rogue often goes in a circle. Soon the elephant is on the trail of the hunter.

There is no reason to kill an Asian elephant for his tusks. They are not worth as much as the tusks of the African elephant.

But the Asian elephant is worth a great deal if he is caught alive. He can be trained to be a good worker. Men who work with elephants grow to love them. They don't want to see their friends hurt.

Today most hunters try to bring elephants home alive. Captured elephants learn to work on farms or in the forests. Or they can be sold to a circus or zoo.

Hunting elephants is a slow and

dangerous business. It often takes hundreds of men and many weeks. First the hunters must find a herd of elephants in the jungle. Then they try to get them into a corral without injury to man or beast.

Once the herd is seen, hundreds of men close in on three sides. As the men move forward, they beat their drums and shoot their guns in the air. The noise frightens the elephants. The beaters keep up the din. They move forward slowly, forcing the elephants together. Step by step, the great herd rolls toward the hidden corral. It may take weeks to get them into the fenced area.

Then the mahout, or driver, must decide which of the wild elephants he will tame. The best ones are the females between two and 15 years of age.

To help in his job, the mahout has

Wild elephants in a corral.

several *koomkies*. These are trained female elephants. The koomkies are put into the corral with the wild elephants. They crowd around one of the wild females and force her into the stockade. Then they jam against her until she is helpless.

The mahout rushes in to tie the struggling elephant. Finally, she becomes quiet.

It takes from two to three weeks to break a wild elephant. Then, as she is given food and water, she becomes tame. Female elephants more than 30 years old are usually freed after the round-up. So are the male elephants.

Elephant hunting is very dangerous. One misstep and the mahout or his helper can be killed in the corral.

Another way to capture wild elephants is by trapping them in deep pits. The hunter finds the broad trail of a herd of elephants. He digs a pit across the trail. Then he covers it with a light layer of logs and branches.

As the elephant swings along the trail, he falls into the pit. Logs crash in on top of him and hold him. The hunter comes back with a tame elephant worker. The prisoner is roped to the tame elephant and is led away.

Sometimes an elephant is badly hurt when he falls into the pit. Or the hunter may catch a female too old to work. Then the hunter lets the elephant go and tries again.

Ancient Warriors

It is hard to imagine an army that uses elephants. Today an army has trucks to carry men and supplies. Jeeps are used to get over rough ground. Tanks push heavy objects and batter walls and buildings.

At one time, elephants were used in battle. When city gates were closed against the enemy, elephants broke them open. Sometimes elephants were used to knock the walls down.

44

At first, war elephants were used to frighten the enemy. Soldiers believed that elephants were sacred. If they hurt an elephant, they expected an unseen spirit to fight back.

Later on elephants were used to carry soldiers and supplies. Usually a driver and four soldiers rode on each elephant. The soldiers carried spears or bows and arrows. The elephant was covered with strong armor. His tusks carried sharp spikes for battle.

Sometimes a tall tower was put on the elephant's back. From this high seat, soldiers could shoot down on the enemy.

When Alexander the Great marched into India, he faced an army of elephants. The kings of India were sure that Alexander's men would be frightened. But, instead of running away, Alexander's soldiers rushed at the elephants. Spears were hurled at them. Flaming torches were used to frighten them. The soldiers even cut off the elephants' trunks. The kings of India and their elephants were defeated.

After the battle, Alexander demanded elephants for his army. He sent them back to his own country. Later his army used the elephants in battle. That was more than 2,000 years ago.

The most famous elephants were those of Hannibal. He was the general of the army of Carthage, in Africa. Although he came from Africa, we believe he used Asian elephants. For the Asian elephant is much easier to train than the African elephant.

Hannibal used his elephants against the Romans. This meant they had to make a long march to get to the city of Rome. At the Rhone River, rafts were built to carry

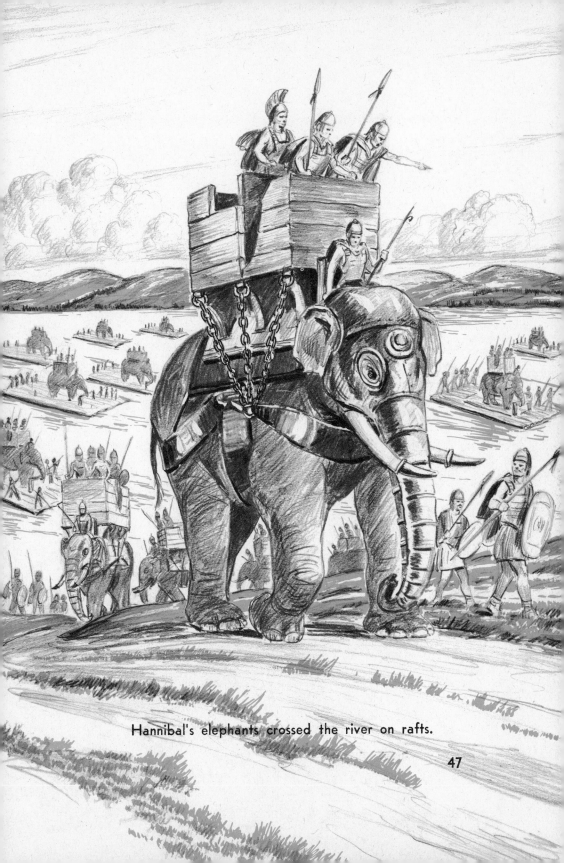

Hannibal's elephants crossed the river on rafts.

the elephants across. Through the Alps, the elephants had to march in heavy snow. Thousands died in the rugged mountain passes.

When the Romans saw Hannibal's war elephants, many were frightened. Others stayed to fight. Their best weapons were burning sticks. The elephants went crazy when the flames came toward them.

Elephants were seldom used in battle after Hannibal's day.

Elephants at Work

Elephants are hard workers. They can be trained to do all sorts of things. In Cambodia, I have seen an elephant carry a whole family to market. The same family will use their elephant to pull out a tree or to plow the fields.

Thousands of elephants work in the forests of Burma, Thailand, Laos and India. At a logging camp each elephant has a special job. Some elephants pull logs through the

49

muddy country. They can even use their trunks to tie knots in drag ropes.

Others load the logs on little railroad cars. This is a hard job, even for an elephant. But I have seen a big tusker balance a log between his tusks and his trunk. Then he heaves it onto the car.

Sometimes two elephants work as a team. Two of them can roll a three-ton log through the forest. Or they can join forces to put logs in a pile.

When the little railroad cars are loaded, another elephant pushes them into position. Then he pulls the chain tight around the logs. Finally, he pushes the loaded train to the sawmill. Machines cannot do this work as quickly or as cheaply as elephants.

When a wild elephant is first captured, he is turned over to a mahout. This is the young boy who trains him. For the

The Asian elephant is a good worker.

elephant's entire life, this mahout lives with him. Day in and day out, they work together. The mahout treats his elephant with the greatest kindness. The elephant learns to obey his mahout and handle him gently. Gradually a deep affection grows up between the two.

A mahout guides the elephant with his foot and knee.

A mahout can tell his elephant when to go forward or backward, when to turn right or left. He can make him pick up things or break branches overhead. Some mahouts have trained their elephants to salute and to kneel.

But the man does not direct his elephant with words. Instead, he uses his knees, toes and heels. With his knees he presses into the elephant's ear fan or his shoulder. Or he taps the elephant with his feet. Each tap or nudge means something to the elephant.

Usually the elephant obeys his mahout. If the animal disobeys, the mahout uses a sharp bar, called a goad. The elephant is very much afraid of this. Indeed, when he sees the goad, he begins to behave again.

Elephants usually work five or six hours a day. They do not work on holidays. They are also free during the long hot summer. On these holidays they are taken to hot weather camps. These camps are on flat land near a pond or river. Here the elephants have plenty of water and grass.

When an elephant is working, he eats an enormous amount of food. One elephant owner told me that every day he feeds each elephant: 11 pounds of wheat flour, one pound of raw sugar, four ounces of butter, 600 pounds of grass, bamboo, branches and sugar cane.

After the day's work, a heavy chain is put on the elephant's forefeet. This keeps him from taking long steps to run away.

A long trailing chain is fastened to his harness. He wears a wooden bell, too. With every step, the bell rings and the chain jangles. They make it easier for the mahout to find his elephant. Each morning he goes out to look for him and bring him in. By ten o'clock they are ready for another day of work.

A farmer in Cambodia told me he would rather have an elephant than a tractor. I asked him why. "Because an elephant finds nearly all his own food," he said. "He never needs repair. And if I take good care of him, he will last many years."

Elephants on Postage Stamps

You learn a great deal about a country from its postage stamps. Every stamp honors some important person or event in that country.

In the United States, we have a stamp that honors George Washington. Another honors Abraham Lincoln. Some of our stamps have honored great inventions. These are important to us.

In Asia and Africa, you see the elephant on many postage stamps. That is because the elephant is the friend and helper of the people.

One of my favorite elephant stamps is from Burma. It shows elephants working in the teak forests. The mahout is sitting on the elephant's back. He directs the elephant to push the log.

There are many elephants in the countries of Indo-China. All of these countries have elephant stamps.

These two stamps are from the little country of Vietnam. They show men going out to hunt tigers. Each hunter is riding an elephant.

One of the first elephant stamps came out in 1942 in Indo-China. It shows an elephant dressed up for a parade. People with a parasol ride on his back.

The Cambodians have several stamps that honor mail carriers. These mail carriers travel by elephant.

The tiny country of Laos has the most beautiful stamps in the world. The artist

who designs them lives in the capital of
Laos. My favorite stamp shows a mother
elephant with her baby.

One beautiful stamp shows the elephant
on parade. This is the way I remember
seeing elephants in Laos.

Notice the mahout sitting on the elephant's head. He is carrying a short, pointed goad. The elephant obeys the goad.

Laos is famous for its teak wood. One stamp from Laos shows the elephant dragging a teak log. The mahout has a goad in this picture, too.

A stamp of India shows two prehistoric elephants. Notice how tall they are. Their trunks and tusks look strange to us.

When Queen Elizabeth of England visited Ceylon, a special stamp was issued. It shows the Queen. And it shows the elephants dressed up for the Queen's parade.

All of these stamps are from Asia. Each one shows the elephant with man. They are hunting, working, parading. The elephant is part of the life of the people of Asia.

The countries of Africa have elephant stamps, too. But the African stamps show elephants in the wild. They do not show men with the elephants. That is because the African elephant is not trained to work with men. He roams the jungle or the grass lands.

Here is an elephant stamp from Africa. It is a stamp of Gambia. You see an elephant all alone trumpeting. He might be calling to his herd.

Take a look at this elephant stamp from South West Africa. It gives a good view of the huge ears of the African elephant.

Now look back at the stamps from Asian countries. You see that the Asian elephant has much smaller ears.

The next stamp comes from French Equatorial Africa. It shows a great male elephant. Note that he is all alone in wild country.

There are many other elephant stamps. For those who are stamp collectors I am listing some of the most beautiful ones.

Elephants on Postage Stamps

Country	Scott Number	Subject
Burma	26, 29	Teak forests
Ceylon	286	Wild elephants
Ceylon	318	Royal procession
Gambia	132-143	Elephant badge of Gambia
India	232	Extinct Stegodon Ganesa
North Borneo	141	Elephant and mahout
Sierra Leone	163	African elephant
Federated Malay States	14-17	Elephants and howdah
Cameroons	239-251	Elephants
Congo	24-25	Hunting elephants
Congo	54-55	Hunting elephants
French Equatorial Africa	197	Great male elephants
Indo-China	213-214	Harnessed elephant on parade
Cambodia	34-35	Mail carrier
Laos	41-47	Elephants
Liberia	35-60	Elephant
Liberia	101, 194	African elephant
Thailand	304, 308	War elephant
Togo	C14	Elephants
Vietnam	63-67	Hunters on elephants

Index

AFRICA

J
599
S544e   642664

| AUTHOR | Sheldon, William |
| TITLE | Junior science book of Elephants |

DATE DUE	BORROWER'S NAME
AP 15 '66	S Jones
MY 13 '66	S. Spear
MY 24 '66	Samuel Reinhart
	312 So. 5th St

PRINTED IN U. S. A.